GW00457230

THE BEGINNING OF THE CATHOLIC CHURCH

A SIMPLE HISTORY

Roy Grant

vi

Christ Pantocrator, Syrian icon, circa 1700.
This is the traditional representation of Christ Omnipotent, which was painted in the apse of early churches from the 6th century and has been repeated to this day by the Eastern Church. Christ sits on a throne, his right hand raised in blessing and holding a book of the Gospels in his left hand.

CONTENTS

PREFACE 1

CHAPTER 1 - THE BIBLE 5

CHAPTER 2 - HISTORY OF THE ISRAELITES 13

CHAPTER 3 - THE SOCIAL AND POLITICAL
BACKGROUND TO THE LIFE OF JESUS 25

CHAPTER 4 - THE APOSTOLIC CHURCH 39

              THE NEW TESTAMENT 51

CHAPTER 5 - THE IMPERIAL CHURCH...........................59

AFTERWORD 65

SUPPLEMENT – SACRED IMAGES...................................75

ACKNOWLEDGEMENTS

I am grateful to my friends Michael Toczek, Michael Sandylands and Professor Gillian Ahlgren, who read my text and suggested improvements; to Simon Francis, for the photographic illustrations; and to Gwen Wiseman who, edited the volume and, through the wonders of modern technology, which is entirely beyond my comprehension, has turned this into a book.

PREFACE

This little book attempts to describe the beginning of the Christian Church from its origin in the faith of the ancient Jews, its foundation by the Apostles according to the life and teaching of Our Lord Jesus Christ, and its establishment as the religion of the Roman Empire. As I have condensed 2500 years of history into five short chapters, obviously this narrative is exceedingly simple and generalised. It is intended for the ordinary Catholic who does not know very much history of this period, to whom I hope it may be helpful.

This is in no way a learned book. I am not a scholar. I have had no academic or theological training. But I was always fascinated by history, and over many years (I am now slightly ancient), I have read books by learned historians. Being a practising Christian, at first 30 years as an Anglican, now 60 as a Roman Catholic, I was naturally interested in how the Church developed through the ages and how it was influenced by historical circumstances. Very much of this has been written from memory.

This writing began as a series of articles for a magazine which circulated among our local church group. I have been advised that it could be of interest to a wider public. Should this be so, I will continue with a second volume describing the next 1000 years of the Church's history during the Middle Ages.

Our calendar is numbered from the birth of Our Lord, and with dates I have retained the classical BC (Before Christ) and AD (Anno Domini the year of the Lord, after Christ). I do not like the modern practice of using 'Common Era'.

Roy Grant

Assisi, August 2022.

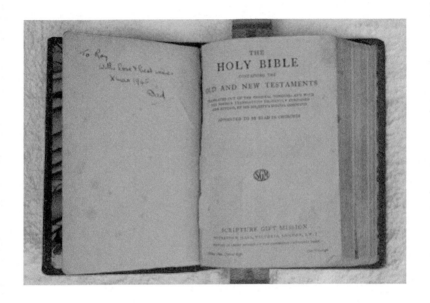

My Bible given me by my father, which I have used all my life, which has the inscription:

"To Roy, With love and best wishes. Xmas 1945. Dad"

CHAPTER 1 - THE BIBLE

The Bible is a collection of books divided into two, the Old and New Testaments. The Old Testament describes the religion and history of the Ancient Jews, called Israelites or Hebrews. The Christian religion is a continuation of the Jewish faith. To understand Christian doctrine, it is necessary to have some knowledge of the Israelites' religious beliefs and practices.

Recent Popes have encouraged the laity to read the Bible. You might find the endless Israelite wars unedifying, though they are often exciting, and the admonitions of the Prophets tedious. There are, though, lovely human stories, as those of Jacob, Joseph, Moses, David, Samuel, Daniel, Ruth, and the Prophet Elijah. There is much beautiful poetry throughout the Bible, especially the Psalms of David (he was a musician and played the harp), which are the basis of the Offices which monks, nuns and priests sing. or say, every day.

The Old Testament is a vast collection of literature which describes the history of the Jewish people, who were unique in the Ancient World for worshipping one god. The God who had created the world and mankind was the God of Israel; he was their Protector, and they were his Chosen People. He bestowed on them the Promised Land to inherit. The Bible tells the story of their journey to the Promised Land, of their battles to possess and protect it; of their successive kings and history afterwards; of their Prophets through the ages, who taught righteousness, admonished kings for their transgressions, and castigated the people when they were led astray to worship the heathen gods of neighbouring tribes. The Prophets foretold the coming of the Messiah, who would deliver the Jewish people from bondage, whom they expected to be a mighty warrior who would deliver them from oppression. Christians, however, identified him as Jesus, the Saviour from sin. The 'Wisdom' books give advice on behaviour and everyday life, and Proverbs of conduct. Some of these proverbs are quoted today without knowing their origin.

The first book, Genesis, begins with wonderful stories which explain basic truths and have a moral message. Almighty God created the world and mankind, represented by Adam and Eve, to inhabit it. Mankind was innocent when created, but then sinned by being disobedient to God, thus losing his innocence. (This is the doctrine of Original Sin and the Fall of Man). Now, no longer a perfect being, man had free will with the power to commit either good or evil. We now know that God did not create the world in seven days but that it developed over countless millennia but the story of the Creation at the beginning of Genesis is a beautiful allegory to explain it. Middle East folklore told of a flood which enveloped the whole earth, so the story of Noah's Flood could have a basis in fact. In the British Museum there are two clay tablets in cuneiform writing of about 1500 BC, from ancient Babylon, of stories of the Creation of the World and of the Flood. The Tower of Babel was probably a ziggurat temple tower common throughout ancient Mesopotamia.

The first five books of the Old Testament, Genesis, Exodus, Leviticus, Numbers and Deuteronomy, called the Torah, the Jews consider their essential books, as they enshrine their faith and rules of religious conduct. The other books were written at different times during their history. Most were in Hebrew, the later ones in Greek.

About two hundred years before Christ, many Jews were scattered throughout the Mediterranean area and no longer knew Hebrew. The Jewish authorities therefore had the Scriptures translated into Greek, the common language throughout the Eastern Roman Empire. This work was made by seventy scholars assembled in Alexandria. and is called the Septuagint (from 70). This was the translation of the Old Testament used by the early Christian Church.

The New Testament consists of the four Gospels Matthew, Mark, Luke, and John; the Acts of the Apostles; letters of Paul to the Christian communities he had founded on his missionary journeys; a few letters by other Apostles; and the Revelation to John, or Apocalypse. These were all written in Greek. The history of the New Testament books will be described later in this series.

As the Christian community in Rome did not know Greek, in about AD 400, at the request of the Pope, St Jerome translated the whole Bible into Latin. He was extremely meticulous, and with obscure Hebrew passages, to get the translation exactly right, he consulted learned Jewish Rabbis. This translation, the Vulgate, is the official Bible of the Catholic church.

The Venerable Bede had translated part of St John's Gospel into Anglo Saxon in the early 700s. The first English translation of the entire Bible was by John Wycliffe, a learned cleric with reformist theological views, in the late 14th century, which however, had a Protestant bias in the translation of certain words. This was condemned by the Church who regarded Jerome's Vulgate Bible as sacrosanct and feared that if the laity could read the scriptures, they would decide religion for themselves, rather than accept the official teaching of the Church. After the Church of England separated from the Roman Church, there were other improved English translations, especially by Miles Coverdale in 1539. These translations were made not from Jerome's Vulgate Bible but from the original languages of Hebrew and Greek.

When the controversies of the Reformation across Europe began, and Protestants were making translations of the Bible, the Roman Catholic Church had their own translation made, the Douay-Rheims Bible, published in 1610. This translation was made directly from Jerome's Latin Vulgate and had notes to explain Catholic doctrine. From this Bible the lessons at Mass were read until modern translations arrived.

In the Church of England, now separated from Rome, Bibles were placed on the lecterns in every parish church for the public to read, and the new printing press made English Bibles available to all. By this time, men of the Middle Class and the merchant class, as well as women, were literate. Someone wrote 'England became the land of the book and that was the Bible'. The later translation, the King James Bible, published in 1611, has most beautiful English language (the same time as Shakespeare, of course). This translation was made by 50 scholars collaborating. The frontispiece states 'Translated out of the original tongues, and with the former translations diligently compared and revised, by His Majesty's special command'. This became the one used generally throughout the world in English speaking countries. It is this Bible my father gave me and which I have used all my life. The quotations throughout this writing are from that Bible as they are made from my memory.

In the 20th century it was decided that the language of the vernacular Bibles was archaic, sometimes difficult to understand, and new translations were needed in modern English. This inspired several new translations. Biblical scholarship today has reached a very high level and all modern translations, both Catholic and Protestant, study the most ancient texts in the original languages of Hebrew and Greek, so they are very accurate.

The holy name of God in the Hebrew scriptures is rendered *Yahweh* (or more accurately YHWH – Hebrew has no vowels). The Septuagint translated this as *Adonis* (Lord) and "Lord" is used in most English Bibles. However, some modern translations, wishing to be accurate to the Hebrew original, use "Yahweh".

The most scholarly ecumenical translation is,

perhaps, the New English Bible published in 1970. This was made by a very large panel of biblical scholars working together over several years For the Catholic Church, Mgr. Ronald Knox laboured for nine years to produce a meticulously accurate translation of the Latin Vulgate, while comparing Hebrew and Greek sources. This was published in 1949 and officially approved for reading of the lessons in church. This has most beautiful English. The more recent Jerusalem Bible, first translated into French but later into English, in 1985, now seems to be more favoured for reading in our Catholic churches. The New Jerusalem Bible is arranged with most helpful instructions to each book.

The Bible is the Word of God. It relates how God revealed himself progressively through the ages, first to the Jews and afterwards to the Church of Christ. It is important that Catholics read the Bible so that they better understand their religion and grow in spirituality.

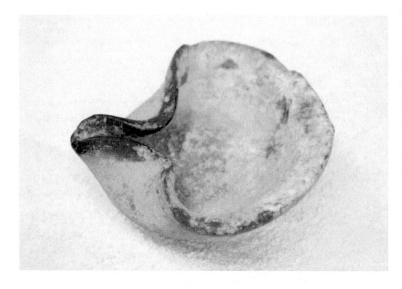

Primitive oil lamp, excavated in Palestine, which archaeologists date 1500 BC, that is 200 years before Moses.

CHAPTER 2 - HISTORY OF THE ISRAELITES

In early history the Hebrew race were called Israelites, as they are throughout the Old Testament; in the New Testament they are named Jews, and this has been their name throughout history afterwards. They were unique in the Ancient World for worshipping one god. The God who had created the universe was the God of Israel, he was their protector, and they were his Chosen People. Their history is described throughout the Old Testament.

The history of the Israelite people begins with Abraham, the father of the Jewish race, about 1900 BC. He emigrated from Ur, in modern Iraq, to Canaan, beside the Lake of Galilee, in northern Israel. (Almost 2000 years later Jesus lived in this same area, and it was here where, at a wedding feast, he changed water into wine, his first miracle). This was fertile country where Abraham lived farming. He had a son Isaac, whose son was Jacob. Jacob had twelve sons who fathered the twelve tribes of Israel. Abraham, Isaac, and Jacob are considered the Patriarchs of the Jewish race.

Events in the life of one of Jacob's sons,

Joseph, brought him to Egypt. You must read his romantic story because it is fascinating, but I have not room for it here, (Genesis chapters 37 to 45). He was clever at interpreting dreams. Pharaoh the King of Egypt had a dream which troubled him, and which Joseph interpreted for him as warning there would be a great famine and it was necessary to store grain in readiness. Pharaoh made Joseph the official to organise this.

When the famine came, Joseph's brothers from Canaan came to buy corn in Egypt, where they were brought before Joseph, now a great official, and he invited the whole family to come and settle in Egypt. There the Hebrews prospered and increased in numbers, so much so that a later Pharaoh ordered all their newly born male children to be killed. To save her son a mother put her baby in a little boat and sent it sailing down the Nile where it landed in the royal garden and was found by the Princess, who adopted the child and brought him up as a Prince of Egypt. He was called Moses.

Pharaoh (probably Rameses II, 1300 BC) enslaved all the Hebrews and set them building his great monuments, the ruins of which you can still see in Egypt. God spoke to Moses, who by now had discovered his nationality, telling him he must lead his people from bondage to a fertile land which he would give them. Moses went to Pharaoh and demanded the release of the Hebrew people. He refused and it took a number of plagues sent by God to convince him, the last being when one night all the eldest sons in Egypt died. The Hebrews were protected, as God had instructed them to smear the blood of a slaughtered lamb on the doorpost of their houses to differentiate them from the Egyptians when God's angel of death passed over. So, Pharaoh at last released the Hebrews. On the last night before their departure, God ordered each Hebrew household to eat a symbolic meal from the slaughtered lamb. This commemoration, named the Passover, has been celebrated every year by Jews until this day. Jesus' Last Supper was a Passover meal, which we commemorate on the Thursday before Easter. (For all this in detail and the future story, which I precis below, read Exodus from the beginning).

Exodus continues the story of the journey of the Israelites to the Promised Land. Moses led them, an enormous number of families with all their livestock, out of Egypt. Pharaoh now decided to send his mighty army to pursue and slaughter them. The Israelites had reached the Red Sea and God caused the water to roll back to create a passageway for the whole company to pass through. But when the pursuing Egyptians in their chariots followed them, God made the waters to roll back again, drowning them. The Israelites continued their journey. On the way God instructed Moses to meet him on Mount Sinai where he made a Covenant with the Hebrew nation as their protector and gave them the Ten Commandments. These were engraved on two stone tablets and placed in a box with carrying poles, called the Ark of the Covenant, and this became Israel's sacred relic. Priests led the daily tramp carrying the Sacred Ark, which at night was housed in a special tent called the Tabernacle, where the Presence of God dwelt, a space so holy that only Moses and the priests were allowed to enter. (In our churches the Blessed Sacrament is kept in a Tabernacle).

The Israelites were always complaining on this hard journey and, when they reached a barren land with no food, said they would have been better off had they stayed in Egypt. The next morning, they found the land strewn with a miraculous bread, called Manna.

The journey to the Promised Land of Israel took 40 years and they eventually arrived about 1250 BC. They had to fight many battles with indigenous tribes to possess it (they had a clever general Joshua) and afterwards to maintain it, but they established themselves.

At first, they were ruled by tribal leaders, but then the people wanted a king. Saul, a mighty warrior, was chosen, but God became dissatisfied with him, and he ordered the Prophet Samuel to anoint with oil David, who then was a youth, as future king. (Throughout history Christian kings have been anointed with holy oil at their Coronation. Queen Elizabeth has said that the anointing at her Coronation deeply moved her spiritually so that she afterwards felt consecrated. The British Coronation ceremony is 1000 years old). The famous story of David is the killing of the giant Goliath, the champion of the Philistines (1 Samuel Ch. 17, v. 23). When Saul was killed in battle, David succeeded as King (about 1000 BC) with his capital at Jerusalem, beginning the Judah dynasty, of which Jesus was a descendant. David was a fine ruler and a valiant warrior. During his reign Israel became an important nation. David wished to build a Temple and bought the land of Mount Moriah, above Jerusalem, for its site; but God wanted this delayed, so the Temple was built later by his son Solomon. By ancient tradition, Mount Moriah was where, almost 1000 years before, Abraham had been prepared to sacrifice his son Isaac (Genesis, Ch. 22).

When Solomon succeeded as King, he ruled as an eastern potentate from his magnificent palace at Jerusalem. He enlarged his territory and acquired great wealth through trade. He gained a reputation as a wise ruler and was respected by other rulers in the area.

Solomon built the Temple on the site David had purchased for worship of God and to house the Sacred Ark, which was still being kept in the Tabernacle tent. It was not a large building, only 115 x 35 ft, as Jewish ritual was conducted by priests inside the Temple while the people congregated outside for worship, women separated from men. The costliest materials were used for its construction, cedar trees brought from Lebanon, elaborate decoration of bronze, silver, and gold. In front of the building was a courtyard with a stone altar on which animals were sacrificed, often lambs, burned to worship God and in reparation for sin. The animal selected had to be perfect, without blemish. (Jesus died on the cross a sacrifice for our sins, which is recalled in the Mass. John the Baptist called Jesus *"The lamb of God who takes away the sins of the world"*, which words we sing in the Agnus Dei.) In front of the entrance was a font where worshipers purified themselves before praying. (We have holy water at the entrance to our churches). Inside, at the end of the Temple, was a raised chancel with an altar where a priest daily burnt incense. (While offering incense, in the later Temple, Zachariah had his vision telling him he would father John the Baptist. Since very ancient times Incense has been used in worship, its rising sweet smoke symbolising prayer ascending to God.) Here, also, was a very large gold seven branch candlestick, the Menorah, which was kept burning constantly. The Menorah became the emblem of the Jewish race and is today the symbol of modern Israel. (It is a very ancient custom to have a light burning before sacred shrines. We have a perpetual light burning before the reserved Blessed Sacrament and we light candles when praying before a statue of Our Lady). Beyond, up a flight of steps, was a small room, the Holy of Holies, the sanctuary for the Ark of the Covenant. Spanning the room from floor to ceiling, were two enormous figures of angels covered in gold, their outstretched wings forming a canopy over the Ark. Here dwelt the Presence of God, a space so holy that only the High Priest, and only once a year on the Day of Atonement, entered to pour out an offering of blood from a sacrificed lamb in reparation for the sins of Israel. At the entrance to the Holy of Holies there was a great curtain. (It was this which was 'torn in twain from the top to the bottom' when Jesus died on the cross.)

When Solomon died, his sons quarreled over the inheritance and the land was divided, the Kingdom of Judah at Jerusalem and the Kingdom of Israel in Samaria. (When in 1947 the United Nations created the modern state as a homeland for Jewish refugees from Hitler's persecution, the

Jews chose the ancient name of Israel).

The Old Testament continues with the history of the kings of both Judah and Israel and their peoples, describing their constant wars with indigenous local tribes and also sometimes with one another, their exile in Babylon, and records the teaching of the successive Prophets through the ages.

In 586 BC the Babylonians, a mighty Power in the region, captured Jerusalem, razed the city including the Temple, and carried off the inhabitants as slaves to their great capital of Babylon. (You should see the massive Babylonian sculptures in the British Museum). The Ark of the Covenant disappeared, no-one knows where. Only 50 years afterwards, the Persians, another of the great Powers in the eastern world, conquered Babylon. Their king released the captive Israelites and allowed them to return home, even giving them money to restore the Temple. So, the Temple was rebuilt, though not so grand a building as the Temple of Solomon. A plaque in the floor in the Holy of Holies marked where the Ark should have stood, though the Presence of God was still believed to reside in this sacred place. It was at this time that the Old Testament books were edited and arranged in their present order.

Two hundred years later, Israel was invaded by

Alexander the Great (330 BC) and afterwards ruled by the Greeks. There was a particularly vicious Greek king who sought to destroy the Jewish religion. This caused a national uprising led by Judas Maccabeus in 160 BC which achieved independence for about 100 years. In 63 BC the country was occupied by the Romans and assimilated into the great Roman Empire, which brings us to the time of Jesus.

Icon of Christ, 6th century, St Catherine's Monastery, Sinai

We do not know what Jesus looked like, as there are no contemporary descriptions of his appearance. This is the traditional image adopted by the Church. of which this is one of the earliest representations. Compare it to the Frontispiece, which was painted 1000 years later.

CHAPTER 3 - THE SOCIAL AND POLITICAL BACKGROUND TO THE LIFE OF JESUS

The land where Jesus was born had been occupied by foreign Powers throughout its history. Israel's religion was an intrinsic part of its national identity and had been preserved inviolate, as had been, to a large extent, its religious social customs. But it had been influenced by these foreign cultures and ways of living. For 200 years Israel had been ruled by the Greeks; only 60 years before Jesus' birth it was occupied by the Romans and assimilated into the Roman Empire. The Romans themselves had adopted Hellenistic (Greek) culture and throughout their Empire had built their cities in Greco-Roman architecture. Throughout the East the common language was Greek. Different nationalities used their own language, of course, for normal conversation, in Israel it was Aramaic. The Romans spoke Latin among themselves. But simple Greek was used between countries to communicate for administration and trade and would have been understood in Jerusalem which was visited by Jewish pilgrims from all over the Middle East. Later, the Gospels were written in Greek.

Jerusalem was a splendid city architecturally. King Herod had built an enormous Citadel, a fortress which included his luxurious palace, set within gardens, and enclosed by a great wall. The upper city contained the palace of the High Priest and mansions in the Roman style for the Jewish aristocracy. Wealthy Jews in Jerusalem had become accustomed to sophisticated, comfortable living. Another fine city was Caesarea, on the Mediterranean coast, the official residence of the Roman Governor, Pontius Pilate, where there was a Roman military garrison, which had an amphitheater, temples, and mansions built around the harbour.

King Herod the Great had ruled for 40 years. The Romans considered him an efficient ruler since he kept the Jews, who were difficult to govern, orderly. He was brutal in suppression of any dissent and paranoid about his personal safety and threats to his throne. His people hated him and to appease them, and probably for his own glory, he rebuilt the Temple as a magnificent building of white marble with gilding in the Roman style of architecture. The Temple church was of traditional design with the sanctuary for worship and the Holy of Holies at the end of the building. Attached were porticos where the Scribes taught and where Jesus preached when he visited Jerusalem, as well as buildings for the Temple functionaries. Surrounding were four very large courtyards, that of the Priests, in front of the entrance, where the altar for the sacrifice of animals was located; the Court of the Israelites, where the men worshipped; the Court for women, who were separated; and the Court of the Gentiles, the only part where non-Jews could enter. There was also a large commercial area, where the animals for sacrifice were sold, and where the money changers operated. (You remember Jesus drove them out, saying *"It is written, my house is a house of prayer, but you have made it a den of thieves"*.) The Temple was the central shrine of Jewry, visited at festivals by worshippers from all over Israel (they would normally go to their local synagogue on Sabbath days.) Hundreds of Jews scattered in countries throughout the Middle East also came to worship at festivals. The whole enormous Temple complex, which covered 19 acres, was surrounded by a high wall with entry gates of silver. In Jesus' day the building would have been only 20 years old, and it only survived 40 years after his death, as I will describe in the next chapter.

It is recorded in the Gospels that Mary took the baby Jesus to the Temple, according to Jewish custom, to present him to God, when the ancient priest Simeon predicted he would be *"a light to lighten the Gentiles"*. Again, when Jesus was 12 years old, when he became lost, his parents found him in the Temple talking to the learned Doctors. In his adult life, Jesus visited the Temple for festivals with his disciples at least three times, and taught in the courtyard there, and, finally, to celebrate Passover in Jerusalem before his arrest and crucifixion.

Herod died soon after Jesus was born. Then the Romans divided the Kingdom. The area of Jerusalem now came under the direct control of the Roman Governor, Pontius Pilate, who was a brutal and insensitive ruler. The Northern part of the country, Galilee, was given to Herod's son, Herod Antipas, to govern. He it was who imprisoned and beheaded John the Baptist. The area of Galilee was where Jesus mostly conducted his ministry.

The Romans throughout their Empire permitted their subject peoples to continue their traditional way of living, their religion and often their government, provided there was no dissent against Roman occupation. In Jerusalem, the High Priest and Sanhedrin, the high religious council, were allowed to govern, though the High Priest had to be approved by the Roman Governor. He and his council were anxious to avoid any conflict with the Roman authorities, lest their limited autonomy be taken away.

In the Jewish religion there were three main groups:

• The Sadducees included the High Priest,

most of the Sanhedrin, and the aristocratic families. They were conservative in their faith, acknowledging only the Torah but not the later books in the Old Testament. Popularly they were often criticized for being political and corrupt.

- The Pharisees were the reformist party. They were exceedingly pious and meticulous in their precise observance of the religious rules and regulations. They were greatly respected by the people. Associated with them were the Scribes, who were experts in interpreting the Scriptures.

- The Essenes were extreme ascetics who considered the Temple priesthood corrupt and some removed themselves from society to form isolated monastic communities.

There was also a national terrorist movement who lived in the hills and sometimes caused uprisings against the Roman occupation. When caught they were brutally executed.

All we know about Jesus comes from the Gospels. There are only two other historical records, brief references to him by the Roman historian Tacitus, and by the Jewish historian Josephus. Jesus' dates can only be worked out by comparing the known dates of the rules of Herod the Great, Caiaphas the High Priest, and Pilate. From this, it is assumed that Jesus was born in 4 BC (so the monk who worked out our calendar, which is supposed to date from the birth of Christ, got it slightly wrong) and that he was crucified around 30 AD.

The Roman authorities ordered a census for which everyone had to travel to register at their tribal city, so Joseph had to travel to Bethlehem, the birthplace of King David, with Mary, his pregnant wife. The city being packed with visitors, there was no room available for rent, so they were forced to sleep in a stable, and here Mary delivered her baby Jesus, and shepherds came to worship him. The family stayed on in Bethlehem for a time afterwards and Wise Men from the East, led by a star, came seeking him to pay homage. These probably were Zoroastrians from Persia who were famous in the Ancient World for their knowledge of astronomy. The Wise Men presented the child Jesus with rich offerings of gold, frankincense, and myrrh. Myrrh was a very costly ointment used to prepare the dead for burial. These gifts had a significant symbolic meaning: Gold signified a king, incense a priest, and myrrh Jesus' death and burial.

They had gone first to Herod's palace in Jerusalem, but were directed to Bethlehem, as this location had been foretold by the Prophet Micah.

Herod intended to kill the child, ordering all the babies in Bethlehem slaughtered. But Joseph escaped with Mary and the baby Jesus, fleeing to Egypt until Herod's death, which occurred shortly afterwards.

Jesus lived as a boy in the small village of Nazareth in the northern hills of Galilee. It was a large family as his foster father Joseph had been a widower when he married Mary and had children from his previous marriage. Besides Jesus, there were four boys, James, Joseph, Judas, and Simon, (afterwards James became an important leader in the Christian community) and girls, whose names are not given. Joseph worked as a carpenter and taught Jesus that trade. His mother Mary was related to John the Baptist's family. Jesus must have been educated as he was able to read the ancient Hebrew scroll at his local synagogue and afterwards expounded from it, pointing out that Isiah's prophesy therein recorded concerned himself. He knew the Hebrew scriptures intimately and frequently quoted them in his preaching.

In the late 20s AD John the Baptist, Jesus' cousin, emerged from the desert, where he had been living an extreme ascetic life. He began preaching in Galilee, beside the river Jordan, warning of the imminent arrival of God's Kingdom and the need to repent sins and be purified by baptism. His 'hell fire' rhetoric was electrifying, and crowds came to hear him and were inspired to repent and be baptised in the river. Jesus also came and insisted on being baptised. Immediately afterwards he went into the desert for a month, praying and being tempted by the Devil, before emerging to begin his three-year ministry. He was now about 30 years old.

Making Capernaum, a little town on the shore of the Sea of Galilee, his base, Jesus recruited 12 disciples and began an itinerant ministry throughout Galilee and in Jerusalem, occasionally travelling to Samaria and beyond the area of northern Israel. Everywhere he preached the Kingdom of God, healed the sick, and exorcised evil spirits. He claimed an intimate relationship with God as his Father, and the power to forgive sins. He attracted very large crowds, mostly of country people, but also the educated and Pharisees. His preaching style was original; he used homely parables to illustrate his message. Jesus liked to call himself 'Son of Man', a title taken from the prophets Isaiah and Daniel.

Jesus was unconventional in the friends he consorted with, who were not considered 'respectable', as well as women companions, which was contrary to Jewish custom. He was not at all precise in the religious practices which a devout Jew was expected to observe. He was frequently criticised by the Pharisees, who were extremely precise in such matters. Jesus said that his mission was not to the pious but to the outcasts *"to the lost sheep of the house of Israel"*. The Jewish church had developed religious rules of conduct which, if deviated from, rendered the person a 'sinner' to be cast out from the community, and with whom no pious Jew would associate lest he be contaminated. They also had very strict rules of table fellowship. The Pharisees charged that Jesus made friends with sinners and ate with them. In reply to the Pharisees' criticisms Jesus said, *"By your ceremonies you have made the word of God of no effect"*. (I suggest that the prelates who criticise Pope Francis are exactly like the Pharisees. And the historical circumstances are similar. The Jewish church in Our Lord's day was 1000 years old and had developed rules of religious conduct which they considered essential to their religion. The Christian Church has existed for 2000 years and, likewise, over the centuries, religious customs and practices have developed which some think cannot be changed or modified to suit modern conditions.)

Many of the people began to identify Jesus as the Messiah (meaning 'the anointed one' in Hebrew, translated 'Christ' in Greek) foretold in the Scriptures, a national leader who would deliver them from bondage, which they interpreted as freeing them from Roman rule. A few days before his arrest, Jesus rode into Jerusalem on a donkey while crowds waved palm branches in an exultant demonstration, shouting 'Hosanna to the Son of David, blessed is he who comes in the name of the Lord'.

Jesus was thought dangerous, both theologically and politically, by the Jerusalem religious authorities and they decided he must be removed. They arrested him and brought him to trial. As the testimony of the prosecuting witnesses did not agree, and Jewish law required precise verbal agreement, the High Priest questioned Jesus directly: *"Are you the Christ, the son of the Blessed?"*. Jesus replied, *"I am, and you shall see the Son of Man sitting at the right hand of Power".* This was a claim so awful they dared not accept it. They judged him guilty of blasphemy and worthy of death.

The next morning Pontius Pilate, the Governor, questioned him. He, of course, was not interested in the theology charge, but people were calling Jesus 'King of the Jews' and the religious leaders insisted Jesus was a political threat. Pilate, therefore, reluctantly according to the Gospels, ordered him to be executed. First Jesus was flogged. A Roman flogging was terrible. The leather whip was tipped with metal so that it tore into the flesh with every stroke, a torment so savage it sometimes killed the victim. Then he was led forth to walk to his crucifixion. Victims did not carry the complete cross, which would have been too heavy, the upright was already set up at the place of execution. They carried only the crossbar (and I think it is very nice that, after 2000 years, we know the name of the person who helped him, Simon of Cyrene. Mark's Gospel records that he was 'the father of Alexander and Rufus', which suggests they were afterwards in the Christian community). Crucified victims were not nailed exactly in the hands and feet but in the wrists and ankles. It was a most frightful death. You can imagine the agony he suffered (and remember, though he was the Son of God, he was physically a man with all our feelings of pain) that he cried out in anguish *"My God why have you forsaken me?"*

So, church and state collaborated to murder the Son of God when he assumed our manhood. But Jesus offered his agony and torment to God the Father as a sacrifice for our sins and for the sins of humanity for all time.

Terracotta oil lamp bearing the monogram of
Christ, from North Africa. 5th century.

CHAPTER 4 - THE APOSTOLIC CHURCH

Three days after his Crucifixion, Jesus rose from the dead and after his resurrection appeared from time to time to his disciples in his human body, both in Jerusalem and later in Galilee, instructing them to go throughout the whole world and preach the Gospel. Then, he took them to a mountain where after blessing them and promising to send the Holy Spirit to guide them, he ascended into Heaven. Then a heavenly messenger told the disciples that Jesus would come again, descending from Heaven at the end of the world.

At Pentecost the Holy Spirit descended on the Apostles and they began to preach. A great crowd from different countries of the Middle East, who had come to Jerusalem for the feast, were miraculously able to understand them in their own languages. Peter gave an exposition of the Christian faith which converted 3000 people. So began the Christian Church. Doubtless people from Galilee and Jerusalem who had heard Jesus himself preach, hearing the stories of his resurrection and ascension also joined the group of Christians.

The Apostles initially remained in Jerusalem

and sought to convert their fellow Jews. They were persecuted by the Temple officials and sometimes arrested and punished. Stephen, a deacon, was condemned by the Sanhedrin for blasphemy and stoned to death, the first Christian martyr. In 44 AD the Apostle James, John's brother, was beheaded by King Herod Antipas. At the same time Peter was imprisoned, but he miraculously escaped. In 62 AD James the Just, described as 'the brother of the Lord' (he was one of Joseph's sons), who had become a leader in the Christian community, was also executed.

Jewish Christians who lived in the various countries of the Middle East, sought first to spread the message of Jesus in their local synagogues. But they were often repudiated, and, very early in the history of the Church, Jewish animosity developed against Christians, which Christians returned. So, to our shame, hatred of the Jewish race persisted all through history, even until our present generation. It became official Church doctrine that the Jews were a cursed race as they had rejected Jesus and put him death. The Church grew up in the Roman world and sought to minimise the Roman role in the execution of Jesus, putting all the blame upon the Jews. Modern Popes have apologised for Christians hatred of the Jews and strongly condemned antisemitism.

The Christian faith began to spread in the great cultured cities of the eastern Greco-Roman world. Several persons educated in Greek philosophy, and also those from various national religions, who had become dissatisfied with their own faiths, were attracted to the worship of one God as personified in the life of Jesus and joined the Church. They began to spread the Christian faith. Travel was easy throughout the Roman Empire, which had paved roads linking the main cities. Many ships traversed the Mediterranean Sea, which had been freed from pirates. And there were the trade routes linking places far apart. So, the Christian message began to spread over long distances, where small groups of Christians established themselves.

The spread of the Christian message had been greatly facilitated by a young man called Saul. He was a highly educated Jewish Pharisee who came from Tarsus, in modern Turkey. His family was presumably important in their hometown as they had Roman citizenship. Saul had come to Jerusalem to complete his studies in the Jewish scriptures. He stood by and watched approvingly the stoning of Stephen, as he strongly disapproved of this new Christian heresy. Hearing that there was a Christian community at Damascus in Syria, Saul sought authorization from the High Priest to travel there and arrest them. On the way to Damascus, he had a vision where Jesus appeared to him. Instantly converted and now calling himself Paul, he turned from being a persecutor of Christianity to its most passionate preacher. In three missionary journeys, totaling together 10 years, Paul traversed the Middle East, preaching the Christian message and setting up groups, with whom he afterwards communicated in his Letters. In between missionary journeys, Paul travelled to Jerusalem to meet the Apostles. Paul had never met Jesus in the flesh, but he considered his vision made him equal to the original Apostles who had been Jesus' companions, Paul considered the paramount doctrine of Jesus was his sacrifice on the cross for the sin of mankind and his triumphant Resurrection.

There arose a controversy between Jewish and Gentile Christians over the practice of circumcision. Jews thought this essential as it was the law of Moses that male children be circumcised, so that they bore in their bodies this sign that they were dedicated to God. As the Christian faith was a continuation of the Jewish religion, Jews thought that Gentiles must likewise be circumcised. To many Gentiles especially those brought up in the Greco-Roman culture, which honoured the human body and where sport and athletics were popular and practised naked, circumcision was repugnant. Paul, who strongly argued circumcision should not be necessary for Gentile Christians, journeyed to Jerusalem to argue the case before the Apostles. This was the first Council of the Church (48 AD). Some of the Apostles thought circumcision was necessary but Peter adjudicated that it was not, only stipulating Gentiles should lead dedicated, sexually moral, lives.

For the first 20 years after Jesus' death the Apostles had remained in Jerusalem, but as the Church expanded, they moved into the larger Roman world to cities where large Christian groups had developed to provide leadership. John went to Ephesus in Asia Minor (modern Turkey) and Our Lady lived there with him. He was the only Apostle who did not suffer martyrdom and lived to an old age. Matthew went to Ethiopia, Thomas to Edessa in Mesopotamia, and later even to India, Mark to Alexandria in Egypt. Peter went to Rome, the capital of the Roman Empire, the most prestigious location, where he became its first Bishop. A large community of Christians had developed in the capital beginning a few years after Jesus' death, so there was already a loosely organised large community before Peter arrived there. Paul joined him later. He had been arrested while preaching in Jerusalem, but, claiming his right as a Roman citizen to be tried in Rome, he was brought there as a prisoner where he lived under house arrest for three years and was able to receive visitors. Tradition attributes the organisation of the Church in Rome to Peter and Paul jointly (they share a feast day on 29 June). By 70 years after Jesus, the Church progressed vigorously throughout the whole of the Mediterranean, the Middle East, Egypt, and North Africa and was more slowly developing in the western part of the Roman Empire.

Large numbers of newly converted Christians had banded together in groups in many different areas throughout the East. They were zealous in their simple, rudimentary faith. As yet, there were no Christian gospels to guide them in understanding the Christian religion. Therefore, it was necessary to create a central authority for instruction, ministry and organisation. The Apostles devised the system of Church overseers of Bishops, Priests, and Deacons. The Apostles passed on the Holy Spirit, which they had received at Pentecost, by laying their hands with prayer on the heads of the Bishops, who passed this on to Priests in the same manner. The Bishops organised the Church groups, choosing the larger towns as their centers of administration. Deacons provided social services, distributed food, and financial help among the poor, and tended the sick. Women were clearly important in the early church, which was unusual in Jewish society, as many are mentioned by name as leaders in their local church communities in the letters of St. Paul.

In 66 AD the Jerusalem population rose in revolt against the Romans. In 70 AD the army of the Emperor's son Titus breached the mighty walls of Jerusalem and razed the entire city, including Herod's magnificent Temple, leaving only one wall standing. (This is the Wailing Wall, where modern Jews pray). All the defenders were crucified, and the city was left abandoned. The Arch of Titus in Rome has sculptures of his triumphal procession where soldiers carry the Temple ornaments with the Menorah. The Temple at Jerusalem, with its rituals and sacrifices of animals, had been the central shrine of Jewry; now the Pharisees adapted their religion for local synagogue worship, and so the Jewish faith has survived until this day. In 133 AD the Jews in northern Israel revolted again. This was brutally crushed, and the Romans evicted the entire population of the country and renamed it Palestine.

The Church had progressed beyond its Jewish origins. Its roots were in the Jewish faith. The Apostles had worshipped God according to the Jewish tradition. When the Son of God became man, he was born into the Jewish race. But Jesus' teaching gave a new understanding of God which extended beyond the Jewish religion and his death and resurrection inspired the new faith of the universal church of Christ which embraced all races and nationalities.

Some Christian converts who came from different cultural and ethnic backgrounds of the Middle East began to mix the Christian message with their previous philosophies and religions and were preaching a hybrid version of Christianity. Known as Gnostics, they produced several writings which the Church condemned. The authorised teaching of the Church was that received from the Apostles.

There was a close brotherhood in the Christian community among all social classes and even slaves, who were an accepted servant class throughout the Roman world. All met together for fraternal meals, where food was shared. The wealthy even sold their property and gave the proceeds to the Apostles for distribution among the poor. At the beginning there were no separate buildings for worship, so groups met together in private houses. The services were simple with extemporary prayers, readings from the Old Testament, and later from the Christian Gospels, with a homily on the life and teaching of Jesus, which the priest had learned from the teaching passed on by the Apostles. This was followed by the Eucharist for those who had been baptised. Records indicate that the

Eucharist was always central to Christian worship. Later, the Church authorities composed formal prayers for the services. When church buildings were erected, ceremonies for worship developed, which in time became elaborated, often copied from etiquette in secular courts.

Christians were always subject to persecution by the authorities, so they kept a low profile. But when they grew in numbers, it was impossible that they should escape notice, and the state began to consider them subversive. Though the Romans permitted their subject people to worship their own gods, they required, as an act of loyalty to the state, the worship of the Roman Emperor, who was deified, by offering a pinch of incense before his statue. To refuse was treason, punishable by death. Christians could not in conscience perform this ritual since it constituted idolatry. In all cities of the Empire the Romans had built amphitheaters where lavish free entertainment was provided for the populace, mostly bloody spectacles. Gladiators fought to the death, and lions and exotic animals were imported and, after being starved, were driven into the arena to kill criminals. Many Christians suffered death courageously in this way. Besides these individual martyrdoms, there were also periods of official persecution when very large numbers of Christians were slaughtered. In 64 AD there was a fire which destroyed the city of

Rome, for which Emperor Nero blamed the Christians. Almost the whole of the Christian community in Rome were rounded up and killed in horrible ways. Peter the Bishop was crucified. He said he was not worthy to die in the same manner as his Master and asked to be crucified upside down. Paul, being a Roman citizen, was beheaded. Afterwards the Church in Rome recovered, but several of the Popes afterwards suffered martyrdom, as did many Bishops and humble Christians throughout the Empire. Martyrs were especially honoured by the Christian community. Their tombs became places of pilgrimage and many of their names are commemorated in our church calendar with the letter 'M' for martyr after their name, and on their feast days the priest wears red vestments to signify their blood. A major persecution was ordered throughout the Roman Empire by the Emperor Diocletian in 303 AD.

But a few years afterwards the fortunes of the Church were to change dramatically, which must have seemed miraculous to those living at the time, when Constantine became Roman Emperor.

Codex Sinaiticus, complete Bible in Greek, 4th century, from St Catherine's Monastery, Mount Sinai, now in the British Library, London. This is a page from John's Gospel.

THE NEW TESTAMENT

At the beginning, the Apostles told the story of Jesus' life and teaching, and this was passed on orally. Nothing was written down. For the early Christians this was not necessary as they expected Christ's Second Coming, the end of the world and the establishment of God's kingdom to occur in their lifetime. When it did not, and the Apostles became old, it was necessary to record the Christian story.

Each of the four Gospels was written at a different area of the Christian community, according to the teaching of those whose name they bear. They vary in detail according to the remembrance and literary style of the writer. Bible historians say that Mark's Gospel is the earliest and dates from just before 70 AD, that is 40 years after Jesus' death. There is a tradition from the second century that this is Peter's Gospel, written down by Mark. Matthew and Luke date from soon after 70 AD.

All New Testament books were written in Greek, the common language. Mark and Matthew are in simple Greek, Luke in highly polished language and his Gospel, as well as his second volume, the Acts of the Apostles, are addressed to an important Gentile named Theophilus. Historians have detected a source, now lost, which is used in each of these Gospels, which apparently had records of Jesus' actual words. Matthew, Mark, and Luke are called the Synoptic Gospels as they are similar in style, recording Jesus' life and teaching, though not biographies in the modern sense. John's Gospel is quite different and is later in date, probably about 100 AD. This is a more theological gospel where Jesus is given long speeches of teaching. It is thought to be a compilation by different followers taught by John. The other books in the New Testament are Paul's Letters to the communities he founded, which are the earliest written Christian literature dating from only 20 years after Jesus; the second book by Luke, the Acts of the Apostles, which describes the activities of the early Church and Paul's missionary journeys; and the Revelation of John. This book describes the New Jerusalem which was to come at the end of the world, containing rich symbolism, some of which to us is obscure but which would have been understood by contemporaries. This book, dating from about 100 AD, was meant to encourage Christians who at that time were undergoing persecution. Although these books were used in different areas of the Church by100 AD, their collection together was not made and authorised until 367.

Writings in the Ancient World, the Hebrew scriptures and the classics of Greece and Rome, were written on papyrus scrolls, which were kept in canisters and unrolled for reading. Christians invented the codex, that is the form of the modern book, which was much more convenient. Thousands of papyrus fragments of Bible books have survived in the hot, dry climate of the East. Christians began to write their books on vellum, that is treated animal skins, which survive for centuries. The two oldest complete manuscripts of the Bible we have are the Codex Synaiticus, originally from the Monastery of St Catherine, Mount Sinai, now in the British Library, and the Codex Vaticanus in the Vatican, both dating from the fourth century.

Ivory fragment depicting the head of Christ.
Byzantine, 6th century, probably from Constantinople and dates from only 150 years after Emperor Constantine built his city there.

Byzantine bronze cross, 6th century, excavated in
the Egyptian desert. Worn by an Egyptian Christian
1500 years ago, I now wear it around my neck.

Pilgrim tokens given to those who came to
venerate Christ's cross after Emperor Heraclius
recovered it from the Persians in 630 AD.

CHAPTER 5 - THE IMPERIAL CHURCH

The situation of the persecuted Christian Church changed dramatically when Constantine the Great became Emperor of Rome. In AD 313 he fought his rival to gain the Western part of the Empire and he attributed his victory to the Christian God. The night before his final battle he had a dream in which he saw a cross in the sky and heard the words 'In this sign you will conquer'. The next day he had the Christian emblem painted on the shields of his soldiers and won the battle. Then he went on to defeat his rival in the East and in 323 became sole Emperor of the great Roman Empire, which comprised the greater part of the then known world, the whole of the Mediterranean (except for Persia, modern Iran, and Iraq), Egypt, North Africa, and Europe.

Constantine issued a decree giving freedom of worship to Christians, and afterwards sponsored the Church throughout his reign. In a later reign Christianity became the official religion of the Roman Empire. So now the Church was not only free to operate openly, but it was also granted favour by the Emperor. Though this brought tremendous advantages for organisation and prosperity, the Church now lost something of its moral integrity as afterwards it was wedded to the secular state. Constantine and the Eastern Emperors after him expected to control the

Church and, in Europe later, Christine Kings expected the Church to support them, so that throughout history the Church became entangled in secular politics and sponsored national wars.

Constantine built splendid Basilicas and churches in Rome, including St Peter's Basilica, over his tomb (not the present building, of course, which is only 500 years old) and St Paul's Outside the Walls on the site of his martyrdom, and gave the Lateran Palace for the official residence of the Bishop of Rome. He sent his mother Helena to the Holy Land to build churches on sites connected with Christ. Among these were the Church of the Holy Sepulchre in Jerusalem, though the building has been destroyed and rebuilt several times through the ages, and the Church of the Nativity at Bethlehem, which remains more or less the original building. Helena also discovered several relics of Jesus including Jesus' Cross, the famous relic of Christendom, and other items of the Passion (many of which are now in the Church of Santa Croce in Jerusaleme, near St John Lateran, in Rome.) Jesus' Cross was kept at the Church of the Holy Sepulchre in Jerusalem but was later stolen by the Persians when they conquered Jerusalem. Emperor Heraclius won it back in 630 and returned it there, and worshipers came in large numbers to a ceremony to venerate it. The Feast of the Exaltation of the Holy Cross on 14

September commemorates this. Some small pieces were cut off the Cross and distributed throughout Christendom.

Because the greater part of the Roman Empire was then situated in the East, Constantine decided to make his capital at a little town called Byzantium, now Istanbul. This was at the crossroads between East and West and had a perfect natural harbour. Here he built a most splendid city which he called after himself Constantinople, whose beauty and magnificence astonished foreign visitors. This was named 'New Rome' and throughout history its inhabitants called themselves 'Romans'. Modern historians refer to the Eastern Empire and its culture as 'Byzantine'. Christianity was thriving throughout the Eastern Empire, where bishops and theologians studied the doctrines of the faith. Constantinople therefore became the center of the Church in the East and seat of the Patriarch.

A theological controversy arose in the Eastern part of the Empire concerning God the Son when he became man, called the Arian heresy, after the name of an Alexandrian priest who propounded it. Simply expressed it stated that God the Son was created by the Father and not coeternal with him. This became highly contentious and was argued with venom, not only by bishops and theologians but even by educated

Christians, who in the great cities of the Greco-Roman area, had inherited the culture of ancient Greek philosophy. Constantine did not understand theology, though he had a bishop who advised him, but his plan in sponsoring the Church was to have a religion which would unify his Empire, so he did not want dissent. He ordered a Council of all the bishops at Nicaea in Turkey in 325, himself taking the chair (though he was not yet baptised). Arianism was condemned and the Council decided a precise definition of the Christian faith, the Creed which we say every Sunday at Mass. There is also another simpler definition, called the Apostles' Creed, which was used at Baptisms, dating from about 400, which we say on the cross at the beginning when we recite the Rosary.

Other controversies arose later which were likewise decided at Ecumenical Councils, that is councils of all the bishops of the Church. In 435 at Ephesus Mary was proclaimed Mother of God, rather than just Mother of Christ, which some theologians wanted to name her. A major theological controversy concerning Christ's nature when he became man was decided at the Council of Chalcedon in 451. Some theologians had argued that when Christ took on our manhood his nature was wholly divine, and he only appeared to be human (called Monophysite). The Council decided that he had two equal distinct natures, human and divine, so that while remaining fully God he was wholly man. Some Eastern Churches, such as the Coptic Church in Egypt, did not accept the decisions at these Councils and broke away, and to this day remain small national separate churches. The great theologians of this period are St Jerome, who lived in Bethlehem and translated the Bible from Greek into Latin, St Ambrose, Bishop of Milan, and St Augustine, one of the greatest Doctors of the Church, who became Bishop of Hippo in North Africa.

As the extent of the Roman Empire was so vast, it had been decided to create a separate Emperor for the Western part, junior to the Eastern Emperor at Constantinople. While the Eastern Empire was securely governed, by the late 300s the Western Empire was disintegrating as invading barbaric northern tribes of Goths, Huns and Vandals began to invade, taking over territory to settle with their families. It was no longer strategically convenient for the capital of the Western Empire to be in the ancient capital of Rome, so it was moved first to Milan and later to Ravenna, which was thought more secure as it was on the coast with a fine harbour and was surrounded by marshes. With the Emperor absent, the Bishop of Rome became the city's ruler. The Roman Empire in the West eventually came to an end in 476. The immigrant tribes gradually established themselves, became civilised and developed more or less the countries of Europe we know today.

The city of Rome had remained well governed and strong throughout the political and social turmoil, chiefly through the leadership of the Pope. Added to the very large community there were small Christian groups surviving throughout Europe from the former Empire. Now the newly arrived tribes became converted and the bishops of the countries they established naturally gave allegiance to the Bishop of Rome as Peter's successor. Thus was fulfilled Christ's saying "You are Peter, and, on this rock, I will build my Church".

AFTERWORD

The Christian community, East, and West was one Church for the first 1000 years of its history. But from the beginning, East and West gradually grew apart. There were several causes.

- The geographical distance between them.

- The division for administrative government of the Western from the Eastern Empire.

- Their church rules and customs developed separately.

- Their language in worship was different. In the Eastern Empire they spoke Greek. The church worship was in Greek and their Bible was in Greek. From the year 400, the Western church in Rome adopted Latin for its worship. (Kyrie eleison, Christe eleison – 'Lord have mercy, Christ have mercy' in our modern Mass is Greek and is a survival from the ancient Greek liturgy). At the same time, the Pope ordered the Bible to be translated into Latin, and Latin became the language of learning and scholarship.

- While the Bishop of Rome was accorded honour as the successor of St Peter, his overall rule was never accepted in the East, where they had a tradition of collegiality between bishops. Their major bishoprics were founded by all the other Apostles, Rome was the only Apostolic bishopric in the West. When the Pope began to claim jurisdiction over the entire Church, this was always resisted by the East.

In 1054, there was an absolute split, caused ostensibly by a theological dispute, but actually over Church politics. Attempts afterwards to heal the schism always failed. The result is the Roman Catholic Church in the West and the Orthodox Church in the East. The separated Orthodox Church retains, of course, the Apostolic Succession and Sacraments. Recent Popes have created friendly relations with the Orthodox Church, but the schism remains. Some national branches of the Eastern Church are in communion with the Roman Catholic Church but continue to use their ancient traditional liturgies in worship.

Painted processional cross. Italian from Arezzo, circa 1280

This is one of the early representations of Christ crucified where he is shown, not in the suffering pose, but as having triumphed over death. On either side are the traditional images of Mary and John. At the bottom, an unusual feature, is Peter's denial. At the four corners on either side are the traditional emblems of the Evangelists as four winged creatures: Matthew a man, Mark a lion, Luke an ox, John an eagle. This symbolism is taken from a vision of the Prophet Ezekiel and also from the book of Revelation of John.

The Virgin of the Sign. Russian icon, 18th century.

This image of Mary is so called as it illustrates Isaiah's prophesy 'Therefore, the Lord himself shall give you a sign: Behold a virgin shall conceive, and bear a son, and shall call his name Immanuel. (Isaiah Ch. 7, v. 14). Mary raises her hands in prayer. Her Divine Son is represented in a roundel on her breast. The earliest representation of this image, in the Catacombs in Rome, dates from the 4th century. Raising one's hands in prayer is a very ancient custom, going back at least 3000 years. The priest does so at the altar, as do we when we say the Lord's Prayer.

73

SUPPLEMENT – SACRED IMAGES

For Catholics, holy images are normal, a part of our religious devotion. But there were no images at the beginning of our religion, which was born from the Jewish faith. The Jewish religion had no images as they were forbidden by the Ten Commandments given by God to Moses. The Second Commandment states 'Thou shalt not make unto thyself any graven image, or the likeness of anything that is in heaven above, or that is in the earth beneath … thou shalt not bow down thyself to them or worship them' (Exodus Ch. 20 v. 2). The Apostles were Jewish, so there were no images while the Church was influenced by Jewish religious practice.

When the Church expanded into the eastern cities of the Roman Empire, the converted Gentile Christians had no prejudice to images, which were common with other religions in their culture. It is recorded that in the mid-300s panel pictures of Jesus and St Peter were on sale in the markets. A relation of Emperor Constantine bought a picture of Jesus, but her Bishop confiscated it, saying 'images were a heathen custom'. So, it seems that Christian images arose from the devotion of the faithful, rather than the official Church authorities. The newly converted Christians regarded Jesus and his mother Mary as 'family' and they wanted likenesses of them in their homes, rather like we in the modern world keep family photographs. These panel pictures of Jesus and Mary became popular in the Eastern Church and remain so until this day. They are called icons, a Greek word which means image,

Early Christian art, paintings on the walls of the catacombs in Rome, where early Christians were buried, mostly date from between AD 250 to 300. There are also sculptures of Christian subjects on sarcophagi from this time. In the very earliest portrayals of Christ, he is presented as the Good Shepherd.

In the early days of the Church, there were no church buildings for worship, so the community met together for Mass in private houses. When Constantine became Emperor and sponsored the Church, however, he built splendid churches and, soon afterwards, they began to be decorated with murals and mosaics depicting Bible stories and images of Jesus and Mary and the saints. From about AD 500 it became general for large churches throughout the Eastern Roman

Empire to be decorated lavishly with glorious, glittering mosaics, and from that time forward images proliferated. The earliest depictions of Christ show him without a beard as a young man in the Roman manner. But from about the year 500 he has a beard, and this became the traditional image. In the apse of these great churches, Christ is shown in heaven, sitting on a throne, blessing with his right hand, and holding the book of the Gospels in his left. But there are no representations of the Crucifixion. In the Roman world crucifixion was a shameful death, the criminal penalty for slaves, and though Christ had died in this way, it did not seem polite to so depict him. So, they preferred to present the image of Christ in the glory of heaven. Prominent in church decoration was the image of Mary, Mother of God. She is presented seated on a heavenly throne, her infant Divine Son on her lap, his right hand raised in blessing.

Though a plain cross was general from the beginning, except for one or two rare examples, the figure of Christ crucified does not appear much before AD 1000, in painted murals and, in the West, in sculpture. The early representations of Jesus crucified show him as the Son of God having triumphed over death, his head upright and his eyes open, not in a suffering pose. Largely through the teaching of St Francis, who emphasised Jesus' humanity and that in his human body he suffered physical pain, from the 13th century, Jesus is shown in the attitude of suffering with his head bowed. Crucifixes afterwards became more naturalistic, which is the familiar image today.

The organisation of the Church in the West developed more slowly than in the great cities of the Eastern Roman world, though Rome had splendid churches since the day of Constantine. From the 1100s the great cities in Europe, particularly in France and in England, began to build cathedrals and monastic churches which were decorated with murals of Bible stories, and images of Jesus, Mary, and the saints. These pictures illustrated the faith for simple peasants who could not read. Sculptured statues often decorated the facades of cathedrals, and statues carved in either stone or wood of Our Lady or popular saints, painted realistically in colour, adorned every parish church. Cathedrals had a special chapel dedicated to Mary, the Lady Chapel. Devotion to Mary was an important feature of medieval spirituality both with learned clerics, and also, in an intimate, homely way, with the common people.

Thus, images became a natural part of our religion and an aid to devotion.

The Eastern Church is very traditional and has perpetuated throughout the ages the same sacred images they first adopted in the sixth century. In ancient Greek and Russian Orthodox churches are wonderful examples expressing an awesome holiness. Unlike the Western Church, in the Orthodox Church there are no statues, images are always flat in either mosaic or fresco, though there are small ivory carvings in relief.

In the Western Church the manner of portraying holy images changed according to the artistic fashions of the age. This art has greatly enriched our Christian culture. Though much has been lost because of the ravages of wars and political and sectarian destruction, an astonishing amount of sacred art remains. Some is still in its original position in churches, the rest preserved in galleries and museums and in private collections. Besides the wonderful art created by famous Masters, there are many beautiful objects surviving from humble craftsmen whose names will never be known.

But the work they created for the glory of God by the skill of their hands remains to inspire and delight us centuries after their death.

Printed in Great Britain
by Amazon

84161364R00058